Carry On

POETRY BY YOUNG IMMIGRANTS

Illustrated by Rogé

Translated by Susan Ouriou

OWLKIDS BOOKS

Preface

For the past few years, I have had the good fortune to run creative writing workshops for newcomers at a high school in Outremont, Quebec. As the students progressed, written wonders began to take shape. My friend Kim Thúy was so moved by their work that she put me in touch with the brilliant artist Rogé, who painted the portraits that appear alongside various students' poems in this book. What you now hold in your hands is the fruit of those many encounters and the sum of much love. Thank you and bravo to the students, my migrant poets, who know their way to the heart.

Simon Boulerice
NOVELIST, POET, AND CHILDREN'S BOOK AUTHOR

This book is a collective embrace among people who have touched my forehead, my eyes, my cheek, my shoulder, my elbow, my belly . . . and, above all, the heart of the ten-year-old girl I used to be, sitting at a desk in a new country that I would make my own.

In this collection, you will find the beauty of which we humans are capable.

There were continents and oceans
volcanoes and mountains
tears and fears
before the route to your heart became clear

Quebec, my dear treasure
I would travel that same path wherever
to wend my way to you
find refuge beneath your roof

in our nest so fair
till noon I embrace you there
till midnight I breathe in your air
one night, ten nights, a thousand we share . . .

we have lost count.

Kim Thúy
NOVELIST AND SHORT STORY WRITER

Pierre Elliott Trudeau Airport
Everywhere everything unfamiliar and new
Snow falling
Wind gusting
People passing

I couldn't get my head around
The changes in my fate to come

What waits for us in this place?
What path will my life take?

Dimitri Dogot

(Moldova)

Kourosh Mohammadzadeh

(Iran)

There are people beside me
Such a comfort
Like steaming hot chocolate

Iran is far from me
I contemplate it only
On a map of the world

At heart, I'm nearby
Only a hand's width away
From my native land

Kourosh Mohammadzadeh

(Iran)

I tossed out my twelve years

My old memories

My old friends, my old country

My cocoon, my life's weave

I have new years

Now I advance

Slashing my chrysalis

Dohee Kim

(South Korea)

I remember my city
Little and noisy
I remember its streets, its parks
Small but adorable

I remember the synagogues
The churches and mosques
Before my eyes a market
The scent of fruit and vegetables
Of every kind

The friends I loved to talk to
To play with during breaks
The young, funny teacher I learned from

But now, for me
All that is gone

Ariel Kegeles

(Israel)

Maria Alejandra Sotelo Rodriguez
(Colombia)

In the Philippines, holidays are extravagant
Booming and loud
Fireworks in hands

Here, celebrations are subdued
But my hands are intact

I had to abandon my friends and family

A year ago, I left

On Quebec's holiday
I learned the name of a new flower
Fleur-de-lis

Olhin Natolla
(Philippines)

The firefly sparkles in the dark
The noisy child watches it

He sees that in darkness
There is light
Even here
Far from Uruguay

I have gained the future
I have lost the past

I draw on this new source of light

Hernan Farina Forster
(Uruguay)

Life is full of memories
Good and bad alike
Bad: puffing on cigars
Good: you, my Pakistani friend

Of Pakistan, I remember
The invitation to your brother's wedding
The jokes we laughed at together
The first place I drew applause
And the time I broke a window

Sometimes at the end of the day
My disappointment looms large

No longer will I make
New memories with you

Mustafa Qureshi

(Pakistan)

Daniil Kondratenko
(Ukraine)

I leave my small country
With my family
Hope lies here in Quebec
Life will be simpler

I will come to this new country
Far from friends who were close to me
A new life will begin

I envision a country
Unlike Moldova in identity
I have new friends to meet
As in a game of hide-and-seek

Valeriu Meleca
(Moldova)

Chayma Medouni

(Algeria)

My parents panic
My sister and I oblivious
We take our last selfies
I see my aunt and my grandparents
In tears

Cruel distance
Overwrought sorrow
A drama queen's tragedy
I'll never see them agaaaaaaaain

Thank you, FaceTime
For showing me their tear-streaked faces
Even here in Canada

Arad Panahi

(Iran)

Immigration is heartache
But a lucky break too

I had to leave something
Behind in my country
But I learned
A new language

I had to leave my friends and my cousins
But I met other ones

I move on from heartache
Gifted with another language
For a fuller embrace

Dowoo Kim

(South Korea)

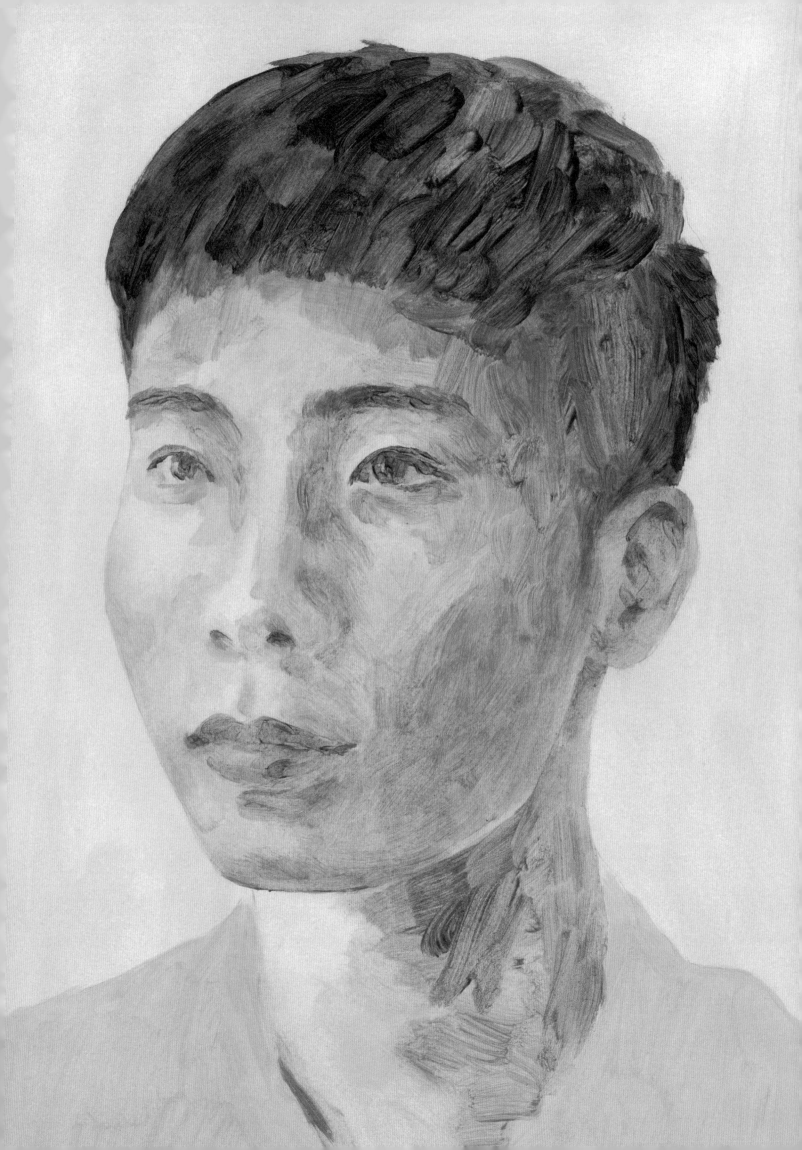

I am a girl from China
Before I left
I was a young bird in a cage
One day through a porthole
A never-seen landscape
Forests, mountains, blue sky

Reaching Montreal
I emerge

Shuning Dou
(China)

Grigor Mihaylov
(Bulgaria)

The aircraft opens
Baggage tumbles out
My father no longer around
Snow: first opportunity

A soothing silence reigns
My past, my future commingle
What will Montreal be like?
Will I be accepted?

A sudden intuition . . .
Disappeared: Latin blood
Escaped: heat
Active: loudspeakers
Deafening words:
"Welcome to Montreal"

My belongings restored
Canada, it's worth it!
The landscape: stunning
Venezuela, we'll meet again . . .

Tommy Zhang
(Venezuela and United States)

I disembark and shiver
I expected less of a chill

The first bite of snow
Such melancholy unknown
In South Korea
Where sidewalks don't ice over

Here I fall

Jiyun Hwang
(South Korea)

I abandoned my life in Dubai
So much sacrifice
For some, I no longer exist
I start afresh

New friends
New memories

I take off my shoes
I am home

Abdul Al Whaibi
(United Arab Emirates)

Antonio Donkov

(Bulgaria)

Who am I really?
Where is my house?

Like birds migrating
I am lost
Far away in a foreign land

Where is my country?
In the cage of my thoughts
Strange dreams surface
In darkness my memory explodes
At this hour my life is a war
I am a lone combatant
I must win

I take a detour
Announce that I am free

Amir Reza Saeidi

(Iran)

The poems in this collection were composed by students, all newcomers to Canada, at the Paul-Gérin-Lajoie-d'Outremont (PGLO) high school in Outremont, Quebec. Several of these works made their way into Bagages, a performance put together by drama teacher Mélissa Lefebvre on identity and the new reality that immigrant students encounter. Traces of the poetry then found their way into Bagages, a documentary film directed by Paul Tom based on Mélissa's work. My friend Kim Thúy joined me for the film's premiere, and we both shed many a tear as we witnessed the resilience of "my" students, their staggering strength, and the radiance of their vulnerability.

When the movie ended, Kim asked to speak to the students about a segment that showed young immigrants calculating the percentage of their Quebec identity compared to their identity of origin. Challenging their beliefs, Kim stated, "No, you are not 40 percent this and 60 percent that, not even 30 percent and 70 percent . . . You are 100 percent Quebecois and 100 percent other. Your identity has multiplied. It is now 200 percent. You are rich in both cultures, not torn between two!" I felt fleeting envy at the breadth and complexity of their identity, since I am limited to one, having only ever traveled for pleasure.

Kim has a gift for celebrating our everyday reality and for successfully connecting people, as she did with me and the brilliant Rogé, whose dream was to illustrate newcomers. This book is the product of much love, driven by the enthusiasm of Myriam St-Denis Lisée, a spiritual care and community involvement counselor, and the passion of PGLO's teachers, especially the extraordinary Nathalie Vézina.

And to my students, I carry you all inside me. Through you, I have grown. Now I'm close to 200 percent too.

Simon Boulerice

Eyes and words are direct paths into people's souls. When we take the time to observe and listen, we are gifted with so many treasures. For me, this book is a pause in the tumult of daily living that leads us to discover the beauty of the other.

For this collection, I had the privilege of immersing myself in the stories of young immigrants. Uprooted from their culture, they have lost their points of reference, and their identities have been shaken. But each one has a light in their eyes that dazzled me. I tried to capture, deep in their gaze, the moment when their truths—both strength and fragility, uniqueness and universality—shone.

Thank you to the young people of Paul-Gérin-Lajoie-d'Outremont high school for agreeing to reveal a part of yourselves so strikingly.

Rogé

Text and illustrations © 2018 Les Éditions de la Bagnole
Illustrations by Rogé
Translation © 2021 Susan Ouriou

Poems by Dimitri Dogot, Kourosh Mohammadzadeh, Dohee Kim, Ariel Kegeles, Olhin Natolla, Hernan Farina Forster, Mustafa Qureshi, Valeriu Meleca, Arad Panahi, Dowoo Kim, Shuning Dou, Tommy Zhang, Jiyun Hwang, Abdul Al Whaibi, Amir Reza Saeidi from a workshop led by Simon Boulerice

Originally published in French (Canada) as *Bagages—mon histoire* by Les Éditions de la Bagnole, Montréal, 2018

This edition published 2021 by Owlkids Books Inc.

Owlkids Books acknowledges the financial support of the Canada Council for the Arts, the Ontario Arts Council, the Government of Canada through the Canada Book Fund (CBF) and the Government of Ontario through the Ontario Creates Book Initiative for our publishing activities.

Published in Canada by
Owlkids Books Inc.
1 Eglinton Avenue East
Toronto, ON M4P 3A1

Published in the United States by
Owlkids Books Inc.
1700 Fourth Street
Berkeley, CA 94710

LIBRARY AND ARCHIVES CANADA CATALOGUING IN PUBLICATION

Title: Carry on : poetry by young immigrants / illustrated by Rogé ; translated by Susan Ouriou.
Other titles: Bagages, mon histoire. English
Names: Boulerice, Simon, 1982- editor. | Rogé, 1972- illustrator. | Ouriou, Susan, translator.
Description: Translation of: Bagages, mon histoire. | Edited by Simon Boulerice.
Identifiers: Canadiana 20200276611 | ISBN 9781771474160 (hardcover)
Subjects: LCSH: Immigrant students—Québec (Province)—Montréal—Juvenile poetry. | LCSH: Emigration and immigration—Juvenile poetry. | LCSH: School verse, Canadian—Québec (Province)—Montréal. | LCSH: Immigrants' writings, Canadian—Québec (Province)—Montréal. | LCGFT: Poetry.
Classification: LCC PS8283.S28 B3313 2021 | DDC C841/.60809282—dc23

Library of Congress Control Number: 2020940656

Manufactured in Guangdong Province, Dongguan City, China, in November 2020,
by Toppan Leefung Packaging & Printing (Dongguan) Co., Ltd.
Job #BAYDC81

A   B   C   D   E   F

Canada Council
for the Arts

Conseil des Arts
du Canada

Canadä

Publisher of Chirp, Chickadee and OWL
www.owlkidsbooks.com | Owlkids Books is a division of bayard canada